INSURANCE BOOK

A COMPLETE BOOK FOR MOTOR INSURANCE

ANUJ BHARADWAJ

Copyright © Anuj Bharadwaj
All Rights Reserved.

This book has been published with all efforts taken to make the material error-free after the consent of the author. However, the author and the publisher do not assume and hereby disclaim any liability to any party for any loss, damage, or disruption caused by errors or omissions, whether such errors or omissions result from negligence, accident, or any other cause.

While every effort has been made to avoid any mistake or omission, this publication is being sold on the condition and understanding that neither the author nor the publishers or printers would be liable in any manner to any person by reason of any mistake or omission in this publication or for any action taken or omitted to be taken or advice rendered or accepted on the basis of this work. For any defect in printing or binding the publishers will be liable only to replace the defective copy by another copy of this work then available.

Contents

About The Book   v

About The Author   vii

Preface   ix

1. What Is Insurance?   1
2. Types Of Insurance   2
3. Types Of Vechiles   3
4. Identification Of Vehicle Category   5
5. Calculation For Vehicle Insurance Premium   6
6. Terms And Meanings   7

About The Book

This Book contains all information regarding Motor Insurance. It will be helpful to People related to Motor Insurance like Insurance advisers,

If you are working or employed in any GI company in any channel, fleet honour.

About The Author

I, Anuj Bharadwaj , is a person having more than 3 years of experience in the BFSI sector.

Therefore I have good knowledge in the BFSI Segment.

Preface

This Book is Beneficial for those who are related to Motor Insurance Business in India only. This Book will help you out to understand different types of in India as per Insurance Companies of India. It will also be helpful for those who want to do some part time Income from Motor Insurance /want to become a GI Agent.

CHAPTER ONE

What is insurance?

Insurance is a tool to cover financial risks of any kind in adverse situations or adverse time.

Many people relate Life insurance with return but actually Life insurance and all other insurances are tool to cover financial loss in adverse situation upto some extent.

Lets understand it with an example.

(God may not do so)

Suppose if your car meets with accident and you have insurance for Your car and you have fulfill and criteria for claim then insurance company will give you something

60% - 80 % of total repairing charges of your car.

So insurance is tool to cover financial risk in adverse situation up to some extent.

CHAPTER TWO

Types of Insurance

In India there are basically two types of Insurance

1. Life Insurance
2. Genral Insurance

Life Insurance: Life Insurance is actually contract of financial Risk cover for customer's family/nominee during any
mis-happening with customer.

Genral Insurance : Every Insurance except Life Insurance falls under life insurance. Genral Insurance is a vast concept. It has more than 200 products .But if we see it percentage wise than

More than 99% of GI is Motor insurance in India due to prevailing laws in India.

But now a day health insurance segment is growing due to awareness of people.

CHAPTER THREE

TYPES OF VECHILES

It is very fundamental for readers to know about types of as per Indian Insurance companies .So, lets begin

the topic.

Basically there are three types

1. Passenger carrying
2. Goods Carrying
3. Misslenious

Further Passenger carrying is divided into two types

a. used for personal use-

1. two wheeler
2. private car

Goods Carrying Vehicle is also divided into-

1. Public
2. Private

    b. Used for commercial use-

    1.Taxi

    2. Route Bus

    3. School Bus/Staff Bus

    2.private

But to understand the difference Between them let us take an example-Any company hired a vehicle T for its

Transportation for one time, then this vehicle was hired by Another company for transportation and then another company/person then Another company/person .It means it is Public.

But if a company buy any vehicle for its transportation
Only then it is Private.

Goods Carrying can be three wheeler or four wheeler both.

Misc: These types of vehicles are used for some specific purpose only .For example-Boring Machine , JCB, Hydra etc.

CHAPTER FOUR

Identification Of Vehicle Category

It is quiet easy to Identify vehicle category by observing its Registration Certificate/Owner Book. If RC is not available, then Screen report from Concern DTO is equivalent to RC.

Things to be observed in RC to identify vehicle type-
1. Vehicle class
2. Model Number
3. Seating Capacity/RLW

CHAPTER FIVE

Calculation for Vehicle Insurance Premium

Common Chart for Easy Understanding

Own Damage Calculation

IDV*RATING = ... - NCB Amount=... - DTD Amount=a+GST=a'

Third Party/liability Calculation

TP Rate +GST=b

Total Priemum= a'+b

Different vehicle in Even Same Class May have Different Rating

Due to its Cubic capacity in Case of Two wheeler ,Private Car, Seating Capacity in Case of School Bus/Staff Bus or Gross Vehicle weight in Case of Goods Carrying.

CHAPTER SIX

Terms and meanings

IDV (Insured declared value) = Value of your car according to
   Your Insurance Company

NCB(No claim Bonus) = When you do not take any claim on your insurance then this Bonus is provided .

Amount of NCB depends upon number of years you did not take insurance but take policies.

If your policy has been expired still you are eligible for NCB

If you did not have taken claim on your policy for 90 days.

DTD (De tariff discount) = Discount provided by Insurance company on own damage part of your policy.

It varies company to company and channel to channel.

www.ingramcontent.com/pod-product-compliance
Lightning Source LLC
Chambersburg PA
CBHW020716180526
45163CB00008B/3121